Short & Fast

THE AUSTRALIAN
Women's Weekly

contents

Most people are time-poor these days, and, as a result, are spending less time preparing meals from scratch than ever before. These recipes use a minimum number of ingredients, but produce maximum flavour. They're perfect for meals during the week, when you barely have time to think, they're healthy and hearty but, best of all, can be on the table in around 30 minutes.

Pamela Clark

Food Director

serves 4 on the table 35 mins

cheese & eggs

kumara, rocket
and pine nut frittata

1 large kumara (500g), peeled, sliced thinly
50g baby rocket leaves, trimmed
⅓ cup (50g) roasted pine nuts
¾ cup (60g) coarsely grated parmesan cheese
6 eggs
½ cup (125ml) cream

1 Preheat oven to 200°C/180°C fan-forced. Oil deep 20cm-square cake pan; line base and sides with baking paper.
2 Boil, steam or microwave kumara until tender; drain. Cool. Layer kumara, rocket, nuts and cheese in pan in two layers.
3 Whisk eggs and cream in medium bowl; pour into pan. Bake about 25 minutes or until frittata is set. Stand in pan 5 minutes before serving. Serve with a rocket salad, if you like.
nutritional count per serving *33.2g total fat (13g saturated fat); 1952kJ (467 cal); 17g carbohydrate; 20.3g protein; 2.7g fibre*

spinach and cheese rolls

Preheat oven to 200°C/180°C fan-forced. Sift 2 cups self-raising flour into a large bowl; rub in 50g chopped butter. Stir in ½ cup buttermilk and ¼ cup water to make a soft sticky dough. Knead dough on floured surface until smooth; roll into 30cm x 40cm rectangle. Sprinkle 120g chopped baby spinach leaves, 1 cup crumbled fetta cheese and 1 cup pizza cheese over dough. Roll dough tightly from long side. Cut into 12 slices; place, cut-sides up, in greased 19cm x 29cm slice pan. Bake about 25 minutes.

makes *12* **on the table** *35 mins*
nutritional count per serving *11.2g total fat (7.1g saturated fat); 878kJ (210 cal); 17.2g carbohydrate; 9.7g protein; 1.2g fibre*

tomato, olive and ricotta tart

Preheat oven to 200°C/180°C fan-forced. Line an oven tray with baking paper. Cut a 16cm x 24cm rectangle from 1 sheet of ready-rolled puff pastry; place on oven tray. Top with ¾ cup chopped semi-dried tomatoes, ¾ cup seeded black olives, ½ cup crumbled ricotta cheese, ½ small sliced red onion and ¼ cup fresh torn basil leaves. Cut a 18cm x 24cm rectangle from another sheet of ready-rolled puff pastry; score pastry in a diamond pattern then place on top of pastry on oven tray, press edges to seal. Brush with beaten egg; bake about 20 minutes.

serves *4* **on the table** *30 mins*
nutritional count per serving *25.1g total fat (12.5g saturated fat); 1965kJ (470 cal); 46.9g carbohydrate; 11.5g protein; 5.8g fibre*

roasted capsicum and prosciutto tarts

Preheat oven to 200°C/180°C fan-forced. Pan-fry 6 slices prosciutto until crisp; chop coarsely. Cut 3 sheets fillo pastry into 6 rectangles each (you will have 18 rectangles). Spray rectangles with oil; stack three rectangles on top of each other to make a star shape. Grease six-hole (¾-cup/180ml) texas muffin pan; press pastry stars into holes. Divide ½ cup chopped roasted red capsicum, ¼ cup chopped fresh chives and prosciutto into pastry cases. Whisk 5 eggs and ⅓ cup cream until combined; pour into pastry cases. Bake about 15 minutes.

makes 6 on the table *30 mins*
nutritional count per serving *13.9g total fat (5.9g saturated fat); 773kJ (185 cal); 4.7g carbohydrate; 10.5g protein; 0.2g fibre*

asparagus and brie bruschetta

Preheat oven to 200°C/180°C fan-forced. Combine 340g trimmed asparagus spears, 1 tablespoon olive oil and 3 thinly sliced garlic cloves in large baking dish. Roast, uncovered, 10 minutes. Cut 430g turkish bread crossways into 6 pieces; place on oven tray; heat in oven 5 minutes. Top bread with asparagus mixture, 200g thinly sliced brie cheese and some fresh thyme sprigs. Bake about 10 minutes or until cheese melts. Drizzle with 1 tablespoon olive oil.

serves 4 on the table *30 mins*
nutritional count per serving *27.3g total fat (11.1g saturated fat); 2249kJ (538 cal); 49.5g carbohydrate; 21.4g protein; 4.4g fibre*

serves 4 on the table 35 mins

800g pumpkin, peeled, sliced thinly
2 baby fennel bulbs with fronds (260g)
125g gorgonzola cheese, crumbled coarsely
1 tablespoon plain flour
2 cups (500ml) cream
½ cup (35g) stale breadcrumbs

pumpkin, fennel and gorgonzola gratins

1 Preheat oven to 200°C/180°C fan-forced. Oil four 1-cup (250ml) shallow pie dishes.

2 Boil, steam or microwave pumpkin until tender.

3 Slice fennel and fronds thinly. Layer fennel, half the fronds, three-quarters of the cheese and the pumpkin in dishes.

4 Blend flour with a little of the cream in small saucepan; stir in remaining cream. Stir over heat until mixture boils and thickens; pour into dishes. Cover dishes with foil; bake, in oven, 20 minutes.

5 Preheat grill.

6 Remove foil from dishes; sprinkle dishes with breadcrumbs and remaining cheese. Cook under grill until browned. Serve gratins sprinkled with remaining fennel fronds.

nutritional count per serving 65.2g total fat (42.8g saturated fat); 3064kJ (733 cal); 22.9g carbohydrate; 14g protein; 3.5g fibre

gnocchi formaggio

500g potato gnocchi
1 cup (250ml) cream
50g gorgonzola cheese, crumbled coarsely
⅔ cup (50g) coarsely grated pecorino cheese
⅔ cup (50g) coarsely grated parmesan cheese
¼ cup coarsely chopped garlic chives

1 Cook gnocchi in large saucepan of boiling water until gnocchi float to the surface; drain.
2 Meanwhile, bring cream to the boil in small saucepan. Reduce heat; simmer, uncovered, 3 minutes or until reduced by half.
3 Remove cream from heat; gradually stir in cheeses until smooth.
4 Return gnocchi to saucepan with cheese sauce and chives; stir gently to combine. This is good served with baby rocket leaves.
nutritional count per serving *39.7g total fat (25.7g saturated fat); 2433kJ (582 cal); 38.3g carbohydrate; 17.3g protein; 3g fibre*

serves 4 on the table 20 mins

bean and coriander
quesadillas

2 x 425g cans mexe-beans, drained, mashed
8 large (20cm) flour tortillas (300g)
2 large tomatoes (440g), seeded, chopped finely
2 fresh long red chillies, chopped finely
½ cup finely chopped fresh coriander
1¼ cups (150g) coarsely grated cheddar cheese

1 Preheat sandwich press.
2 Spread beans over four tortillas. Sprinkle with tomato, chilli, coriander and cheese. Top with remaining tortillas.
3 Cook quesadillas in sandwich press until browned both sides and heated through; cut into wedges. Serve accompanied with sour cream, if you like.
nutritional count per serving *15g total fat (8.4g saturated fat); 1898kJ (454 cal); 49.5g carbohydrate; 23.3g protein; 13.4g fibre*

smoked salmon and mascarpone omelette

8 eggs
½ cup (125g) mascarpone cheese
20g unsalted butter
100g sliced smoked salmon
2 tablespoons finely chopped fresh chives
2 tablespoons finely chopped fresh chervil

1 Whisk eggs with 2 tablespoons of the cheese in medium bowl until combined.

2 Melt a quarter of the butter in small frying pan (base 16cm). When butter is foaming, pour a quarter of the egg mixture into pan; cook over medium heat, tilting pan, until omelette is set.

3 Top half the omelette with a quarter of the salmon, a quarter of the combined herbs and a quarter of the remaining cheese. Fold omelette over to enclose filling. Slide omelette onto serving plate.

4 Repeat to make three more omelettes.

nutritional count per serving *30.6g total fat (16.3g saturated fat); 1496kJ (358 cal); 1g carbohydrate; 20.6g protein; 0.1g fibre*

serves 4 on the table 20 mins

4 eggs
8 rindless bacon rashers (520g)
120g baby spinach leaves
2 tablespoons olive oil
2 tablespoons red wine vinegar
1 clove garlic, crushed

spinach, bacon and poached egg salad

1 Half fill a large frying pan with water; bring to the boil. Break 1 egg into a cup then slide into pan. Repeat with remaining eggs. When all eggs are in pan, return water just to the boil. Cover pan, turn off heat; stand about 4 minutes or until a light film of white sets over each yolk. Using a slotted spoon, remove eggs, one at a time, from pan; rest spoon on absorbent-paper-lined saucer to blot up poaching liquid.
2 Meanwhile, cook bacon in heated oiled large frying pan until crisp; drain on absorbent paper. Chop coarsely.
3 Combine spinach, oil, vinegar, garlic and bacon in large bowl. Serve salad topped with poached eggs.
nutritional count per serving *31.8g total fat (9.3g saturated fat); 1747kJ (418 cal); 0.9g carbohydrate; 32.5g protein; 0.9g fibre*

serves 4 on the table 10 mins

salads

beetroot and fetta salad

440g can whole baby beets, drained, halved
100g mesclun
1 cup firmly packed fresh mint leaves
250g jar marinated fetta in oil
1 teaspoon balsamic vinegar
1 teaspoon dijon mustard

1 Divide combined beetroot, mesclun and mint among serving bowls.
2 Drain fetta, reserving 2 tablespoons of oil. Chop fetta into cubes, divide among serving bowls. Combine reserved oil with vinegar and mustard in small bowl; drizzle over salad.

nutritional count per serving *23.3g total fat (9.3g saturated fat); 1024kJ (288 cal); 8g carbohydrate; 10.7g protein;3.4 g fibre*

char-grilled tofu salad

Halve 115g baby corn; drop into small saucepan of boiling water, drain. Combine corn in large bowl with 100g baby asian greens and 1 sliced large red capsicum. Char-grill 350g sliced firm tofu until golden; add to salad. Drizzle with ⅓ cup asian-style dressing; sprinkle with 1 tablespoon toasted sesame seeds.

serves *4* **on the table** *10 mins*
nutritional count per serving *14.7g total fat (1.8g saturated fat); 995kJ (238 cal); 10.6g carbohydrate; 13.8g protein; 4.7g fibre*

Toast sesame seeds in a small frying pan, over medium heat, shaking pan occasionally, until golden and fragrant, about 3-5 minutes.

teriyaki beef salad

Combine ¼ cup teriyaki sauce and 2 teaspoons sesame oil in small jug. Combine half the teriyaki mixture with 500g piece of beef rump steak in medium bowl. Cook beef on oiled grill plate. Cover, stand 15 minutes; slice beef thinly. Combine beef and remaining teriyaki mixture with 120g baby mesclun, 1 seeded, thinly sliced lebanese cucumber and 2 thinly sliced red radishes in large bowl.

serves *4* **on the table** *25 mins*
nutritional count per serving *10.8g total fat (4.1g saturated fat); 932kJ (223 cal); 1.4g carbohydrate; 29.4g protein; 1g fibre*

haloumi, zucchini and spinach salad

Drain 270g jar semi-dried tomatoes in oil; reserve 2 tablespoons of the oil. Cook 1 thinly sliced large yellow zucchini and 250g thinly sliced haloumi cheese on heated oiled grill plate (or grill or barbecue) until browned lightly. Divide 100g baby spinach leaves, cheese, tomatoes and zucchini among serving plates. Whisk reserved oil, 2 tablespoons lemon juice and 1 tablespoon coarsely chopped rosemary in small bowl; serve with salad.

serves *4* **on the table** *25 mins*
nutritional count per serving *22.5g total fat (8.5g saturated fat); 1618kJ (387 cal); 21.2g carbohydrate; 20.8g protein; 9.3g fibre*

rocket, prosciutto and egg salad

Pan-fry 8 slices prosciutto until crisp; chop coarsely. Cut four hard-boil eggs in half. Divide 120g baby rocket leaves and eggs among serving plates. Sprinkle with prosciutto and ¼ cup shaved parmesan cheese. Serve drizzled with ½ cup caesar dressing.

serves *4* **on the table** *25 mins*
nutritional count per serving *18.3g total fat (4.6g saturated fat); 1117kJ (267 cal); 8.1g carbohydrate; 17.6g protein; 0.4g fibre*

serves 4 on the table 15 mins

egg salad with croûtons

1 medium butter lettuce, leaves separated
250g cherry tomatoes, halved
2 shallots (50g), sliced thinly
⅓ cup (80ml) ranch dressing
4 hard-boiled eggs, halved
75g packet croûtons

1 Divide lettuce, tomato, shallot and dressing among serving bowls.
2 Serve topped with egg and croûtons.
nutritional count per serving 18.1g total fat (4.1g saturated fat); 1099kJ (263 cal); 13.2g carbohydrate; 10g protein; 4.2g fibre

serves 4 on the table 20 mins

potato, prosciutto and pomegranate salad

10 medium kipfler (950g) potatoes,
   halved lengthways
⅓ cup (80ml) lemon juice
2 tablespoons olive oil
6 slices prosciutto (90g)
80g baby spinach leaves
½ cup (125ml) pomegranate pulp

1 Cook potato in saucepan of boiling water
10 minutes or until just tender; drain. Cool, peel;
cut into 1cm pieces. Place in large bowl with juice
and oil; toss to coat potato in mixture.
2 Preheat grill. Grill prosciutto about 5 minutes
or until crisp; chop coarsely.
3 Divide spinach, potato, prosciutto and pulp
among serving plates.
nutritional count per serving *4g total fat
(0.8g saturated fat); 1003kJ (240 cal);
36.1g carbohydrate; 11g protein; 7.3g fibre*

**You need to buy a medium pomegranate
(320g) to get ½ cup pulp. To remove the pulp,
cut pomegranate in half, then hit the back of the
fruit with a wooden spoon – the seeds usually fall
out easily. Discard the shell and white pith.**

roast pumpkin and lentil salad

1kg pumpkin, peeled, cut into 2cm pieces
1 tablespoon olive oil
1 tablespoon cajun seasoning mix
400g can lentils, rinsed, drained
80g baby spinach leaves
½ cup (140g) greek-style yogurt

1 Preheat oven to 220°C/200°C fan-forced.
2 Toss pumpkin, oil and seasoning mix in medium baking dish; roast, uncovered, about 20 minutes or until tender.
3 Divide pumpkin, lentils and spinach among serving plates. Mix yogurt with 1 tablespoon of water in a small bowl; drizzle over salad.
nutritional count per serving *6.9g total fat (2g saturated fat); 794kJ (190 cal); 20g carbohydrate; 9.6g protein; 4.8g fibre*

serves 4 on the table 15 mins

340g asparagus, trimmed
200g sliced smoked salmon
4 hard-boiled eggs, quartered
creamy dill dressing
2 tablespoons sour cream
2 tablespoons lemon juice
2 teaspoons finely chopped fresh dill

smoked salmon, egg and asparagus salad

1 Cook asparagus on heated oiled grill plate (or grill or barbecue) until tender.

2 Meanwhile, make creamy dill dressing.

3 Divide salmon, asparagus and eggs among serving plates; drizzle with dressing.

creamy dill dressing Whisk ingredients in a small bowl.

nutritional count per serving *13.3 g total fat (5.1g saturated fat); 836kJ (200 cal); 1.5g carbohydrate; 18.4g protein; 0.9g fibre*

smoked trout, brie
and cranberry salad

350g trimmed watercress
200g smoked trout, flaked coarsely
110g brie cheese, sliced thinly
cranberry dressing
2 tablespoons olive oil
2 tablespoons cranberry juice
1 tablespoon lemon juice

1 Divide watercress, trout and cheese among serving plates.
2 Make cranberry dressing.
3 Drizzle dressing over salad.
cranberry dressing Combine ingredients in screw-top jar; shake well.
nutritional count per serving 19.8g total fat (7g saturated fat); 1095kJ (262 cal); 1.4g carbohydrate; 19.3g protein; 0.7g fibre

serves 4 on the table 25 mins

seafood

fish cake skewers

Red curry paste is available in various strengths from supermarkets. Use whichever one suits your spice-level tolerance best.

750g firm white fish fillets, chopped coarsely
2 tablespoons (50g) red curry paste
2 green onions, chopped coarsely
⅓ cup coarsely chopped fresh coriander leaves
1 cup (250ml) sweet chilli sauce
peanut oil, for deep frying

1 Process fish, paste, onion and coriander until combined; stir in 2 tablespoons of the sweet chilli sauce. Roll mixture into 12 sausage shapes.
2 Heat oil in large deep saucepan; deep-fry fish cakes, in batches, until browned and cooked through.
3 Skewer each log with a bamboo skewer. Serve fish cake skewers with remaining sweet chilli sauce.
nutritional count per serving *23.4g total fat (4.5g saturated fat); 1802kJ (431 cal); 13.9g carbohydrate; 36.7g protein; 4.4g fibre*

chorizo prawn pizza

Preheat oven to 220°C/200°C fan-forced. Shell and devein 360g uncooked medium king prawns; halve prawns lengthways. Spread four small pizza bases with ½ cup bottled pizza sauce. Top with 12 halved cherry bocconcini, 1 thinly sliced chorizo sausage and prawns. Bake about 15 minutes. Serve pizzas sprinkled with baby rocket leaves, if you like.

makes *4* **on the table** *25 mins*

nutritional count per serving *23.9g total fat (9.7g saturated fat); 2483kJ (594 cal); 57.4g carbohydrate; 34.7g protein; 4.5g fibre*

satay prawn stir-fry

Shell and devein 1.5kg uncooked large king prawns, leaving tails intact. Thickly slice 1 large red capsicum. Heat 1 tablespoon peanut oil in wok. Stir-fry prawns and capsicum until prawns change colour. Add 250ml can satay sauce and 3 thinly sliced green onions; stir-fry until hot.

serves *4* **on the table** *30 mins*

nutritional count per serving *18.1g total fat (4.4g saturated fat); 1672kJ (400 cal); 13.7g carbohydrate; 43.9g protein; 3.1g fibre*

lemon fish parcels

Preheat oven to 200°C/180°C fan-forced. Rinse and drain 425g can whole peeled baby potatoes; halve potatoes. Place four large squares of baking paper on top of four large squares of foil; layer potato and 340g trimmed asparagus on squares. Top with 4 x 200g firm white fish fillets. Drizzle fish with ¼ cup lemon juice and 1 tablespoon olive oil; enclose fish in foil. Place parcels on oven tray; cook about 15 minutes. Serve with baby spinach leaves and lemon wedges, if you like.

serves 4 on the table *30 mins*
nutritional count per serving *9.1g total fat*
(2g saturated fat); 1271kJ (304 cal);
10g carbohydrate; 43.9g protein; 2.1g fibre

spicy fish burgers

Sprinkle 4 x 180g firm white fish fillets with 2 tablespoons peri-peri spice mix. Cook fish in heated oiled large frying pan. Meanwhile, split 4 bread rolls in half, toast cut sides, spread with combined ½ cup mayonnaise and 2 tablespoons finely chopped fresh dill. Separate the leaves from 1 baby cos lettuce. Sandwich rolls with baby cos lettuce leaves and fish.

serves 4 on the table *20 mins*
nutritional count per serving *15.2g total fat*
(2.5g saturated fat); 1726kJ (413 cal);
26.5g carbohydrate; 40.9g protein; 2.7g fibre

serves 6 on the table 20 mins

lemon tuna pasta

500g spaghetti
425g can tuna in oil, undrained
⅔ cup (100g) semi-dried tomatoes in oil, drained
1 teaspoon finely grated lemon rind
¼ cup (60ml) lemon juice
50g baby rocket leaves
½ cup (40g) shaved parmesan cheese

1 Cook pasta in large saucepan of boiling water, uncovered, until tender; drain.
2 Meanwhile, warm undrained tuna and tomatoes in medium saucepan.
3 Combine spaghetti, rind, juice, tuna mixture and rocket in large bowl; sprinkle with cheese.
nutritional count per serving *20.9g total fat (4.2g saturated fat); 2370kJ (567 cal); 63g carbohydrate; 28.7g protein; 5.3g fibre*

serves 4 on the table 35 mins

salmon rissoles

2 cups (185g) instant mash
415g can red salmon, drained, flaked
½ cup (40g) finely grated parmesan cheese
4 medium tomatoes (600g), chopped coarsely
1 cup firmly packed fresh flat-leaf parsley

1 Combine instant mash and 2 cups (500ml) boiling water in large heatproof bowl.
2 Add salmon and cheese to potato mixture; shape into eight patties. Place patties on tray; refrigerate 10 minutes.
3 Cook patties, in batches, in heated oiled large frying pan until browned lightly and heated through.
4 Meanwhile, combine tomato and parsley in medium bowl.
5 Serve rissoles with tomato and parsley salad.
nutritional count per serving *11.5g total fat (5.1g saturated fat); 1492kJ (357 cal); 32.5g carbohydrate; 27.2g protein; 6.4g fibre*

Instant mash is a dried mashed potato mix reconstituted with boiling liquid to give a light buttery flavour. It is available from most supermarkets.

peri-peri squid

800g cleaned baby squid hoods
2 tablespoons peri-peri spice mix
vegetable oil, for deep frying
½ cup (75g) cornflour
⅔ cup (200g) mayonnaise
80g baby rocket leaves

1 Cut squid down centre to open out; score inside in diagonal pattern then cut into thick strips. Pat dry.
2 Reserve 1 teaspoon spice mix. Combine squid and remaining spice mix in large bowl.
3 Heat oil in large deep frying pan.
4 Just before frying, toss squid in cornflour, in batches; shake off excess. Deep-fry squid, in batches, until browned lightly and tender. Drain.
5 Meanwhile, combine mayonnaise and reserved spice mix in small bowl.
6 Serve squid with rocket and mayonnaise.
nutritional count per serving *29g total fat (3.9g saturated fat); 2128kJ (509 cal); 27.2g carbohydrate; 34.6g protein; 0.9g fibre*

calamari rice

1½ cups (300g) jasmine rice
1 cup (250ml) bottled tomato pasta sauce
600g cleaned baby squid hoods
2 cloves garlic, crushed
1 cup coarsely chopped fresh flat-leaf parsley
⅓ cup (25g) shaved parmesan cheese

1 Rinse rice under cold water until water runs clear; drain. Combine rice, pasta sauce and 3½ cups (875ml) water in medium saucepan; bring to the boil, stirring occasionally. Reduce heat; simmer, covered tightly, about 15 minutes or until tender. Remove from heat; stand, covered, 5 minutes.

2 Meanwhile, slice squid thickly into rings. Combine squid and garlic in medium bowl.

3 Cook squid, in batches, in heated oiled large frying pan until tender. Combine squid with rice and parsley. Serve sprinkled with cheese.

nutritional count per serving 4.8g total fat (2g saturated fat); 457kJ (109 cal); 66.1g carbohydrate; 33.8g protein; 2.9g fibre

serves 4 on the table 20 mins

prawns with
avocado and mango

2 small avocados (200g), chopped coarsely
2 tablespoons lime juice
2 medium mangoes (860g), chopped coarsely
800g cooked medium king prawns
80g mesclun

1 Blend or process avocado, juice and 2 tablespoons water until smooth. Place in medium bowl.
2 Blend or process mango until smooth.
3 Shell and devein prawns, leaving tails intact.
4 Divide purées among serving plates; top with mesclun and prawns.
nutritional count per serving *8.9g total fat (1.8g saturated fat); 1083kJ (259 cal); 19.7g carbohydrate; 23g protein; 3.3g fibre*

snapper fillets with
ginger soy syrup

2 medium carrots (240g), cut into matchsticks
2 medium zucchini (240g), cut into matchsticks
4 x 275g snapper fillets, skin on
1 cup (250ml) bottled sweet chilli, ginger and
   soy marinade

1 Boil, steam or microwave carrot and zucchini,
separately, until tender.
2 Meanwhile, score fish skin. Cook fish, skin-side
down, in heated oiled large frying pan about
5 minutes. Turn fish; cook about 3 minutes.
Remove from pan.
3 Add ⅓ cup (80ml) water and marinade to
same pan; stir until hot.
4 Serve fish with sauce and vegetables. Serve
with steamed jasmine rice, if you like.
nutritional count per serving *4.6g total fat*
(1.7g saturated fat); 1304kJ (312 cal);
5.4g carbohydrate; 60.4g protein; 2.4g fibre

serves 4 on the table 25 mins

grilled baby
octopus salad

800g cleaned baby octopus, halved
250g haloumi cheese, chopped coarsely
100g baby spinach leaves
oregano dressing
1 tablespoon ground oregano
⅓ cup (80ml) lime juice
½ cup (125ml) olive oil

1 Make oregano dressing.
2 Combine octopus and half the dressing in large bowl.
3 Cook octopus and cheese on heated oiled grill plate (or grill or barbecue) until tender and golden.
4 Combine octopus, cheese and spinach in large bowl with remaining dressing.
oregano dressing Combine ingredients in screw-top jar; shake well.
nutritional count per serving 40.6g total fat (10.9g saturated fat); 2332kJ (558 cal); 1.7g carbohydrate; 46.9g protein; 0.9g fibre

serves 4 on the table 25 mins

moroccan fish with
almond couscous

1 cup (200g) couscous
1 cup (80g) flaked almonds, roasted
2 tablespoons moroccan spice mix
4 x 180g blue-eye fillets
2 tablespoons finely chopped fresh mint
⅔ cup (190g) yogurt

1 Combine couscous with 1 cup (250ml) boiling
water in medium heatproof bowl, cover; stand
5 minutes or until liquid is absorbed, fluffing with
fork occasionally. Stir in nuts.
2 Meanwhile, rub spice mix all over fish. Cook fish in
heated oiled large frying pan. Break fish into chunks.
3 Combine mint and yogurt in small bowl; stir in a
little water, if you like.
4 Serve fish with couscous and minted yogurt.
nutritional count per serving *17.2g total fat*
(3.1g saturated fat); 2224kJ (532 cal);
42.6g carbohydrate; 49.7g protein; 2.7g fibre

**Any firm white fish fillet, such as cod, bream,
flathead, swordfish, ling, whiting, jewfish or
snapper are all good choices in this recipe.**

salmon with creamy dill sauce

4 x 220g salmon fillets, skin on
1 small brown onion (80g), chopped finely
300ml cream
1 tablespoon coarsely chopped fresh dill

1 Cook fish, skin-side down, in heated oiled large frying pan about 5 minutes. Turn fish; cook about 3 minutes. Remove fish from pan; cover.

2 Combine onion and cream in small saucepan; simmer, uncovered, 8 minutes; stir in dill.

3 Spoon sauce over fish; serve fish with mixed salad leaves, if you like.

nutritional count per serving *48.1g total fat (25g saturated fat); 2517kJ (619 cal); 3.2g carbohydrate; 44.6g protein; 0.3g fibre*

thai broth with prawns

1kg uncooked medium king prawns
350g packet singapore noodles
80g sugar snap peas, trimmed
½ cup loosely packed fresh coriander leaves
50g packet tom yum soup
300g baby buk choy, leaves separated

1 Shell and devein prawns, leaving tails intact.
2 Place noodles in large heatproof bowl, cover with boiling water; separate noodles with fork, drain.
3 Divide noodles, peas and coriander between four serving bowls.
4 Combine 3 cups (750ml) water with the soup mix in medium saucepan; bring to the boil.
5 Add prawns and buk choy to soup; simmer until prawns change colour. Ladle broth into bowls.

nutritional count per serving *2.2g total fat (0.4g saturated fat); 1760kJ (421 cal); 58.1g carbohydrate; 39g protein; 3.8g fibre*

serves 4 on the table 35 mins

meat

chilli con carne

500g beef mince
2 fresh long red chillies, chopped finely
35g packet taco seasoning mix
400g can diced tomatoes
420g can kidney beans, rinsed, drained
⅓ cup coarsely chopped fresh coriander

1 Cook mince in heated oiled large frying pan, stirring, until browned. Add chillies and seasoning mix; cook, stirring, until fragrant.
2 Add undrained tomatoes and ½ cup (125ml) water; bring to the boil. Reduce heat; simmer, uncovered, 15 minutes. Add beans; simmer, uncovered, 5 minutes. Remove from heat, stir in coriander. Chilli con carne is delicious served with warm corn tortillas and sour cream.
nutritional count per serving *12.5g total fat (5.2g saturated fat); 1296kJ (310 cal); 16.9g carbohydrate; 24.2g protein; 6.8g fibre*

teriyaki beef and soba stir-fry

Cook 270g dried soba noodles in large saucepan of boiling water, uncovered, until tender; drain. Meanwhile, heat 2 tablespoons peanut oil in wok; stir-fry 600g thinly sliced beef eye-fillet until browned. Cut 6 green onions into 5cm lengths, add to wok; stir-fry until soft. Add ⅓ cup teriyaki sauce and noodles to wok; stir-fry until heated through. Remove from heat; add 2 cups bean sprouts to wok, toss to combine.

serves 4 on the table *20 mins*

nutritional count per serving *18.9g total fat (5.5g saturated fat); 2245kJ (537 cal); 47.8g carbohydrate; 41.5g protein; 3.8g fibre*

haloumi and parsley crumbed veal

Whisk 1 egg and 1½ tablespoons water in medium shallow bowl. Combine ¾ cup stale breadcrumbs, 60g coarsely grated haloumi cheese and 1 tablespoon finely chopped fresh flat-leaf parsley in another medium shallow bowl. Dip 4 x 150g veal cutlets in egg mixture then coat in cheese mixture. Refrigerate 10 minutes. Heat 2 tablespoons vegetable oil in large frying pan; cook veal until browned lightly and cooked through, drain. Veal would go well with a mixed green salad and lemon wedges.

serves 4 on the table *35 mins*

nutritional count per serving *15.3g total fat (3.8g saturated fat); 1271kJ (304 cal); 80g carbohydrate; 33.2g protein; 0.5g fibre*

italian-style lamb cutlets

Cut a small horizontal slit in the side of eight french-trimmed lamb cutlets. Combine 100g firm crumbled goats cheese, ¼ cup finely chopped sun-dried tomatoes and 2 tablespoons finely shredded fresh basil in medium bowl. Press cheese mixture into lamb pockets. Wrap each cutlet with a thin slice of prosciutto. Cook cutlets in heated oiled large frying pan until cooked through. Good served with half a baby cos lettuce and drizzled with your choice of dressing.

serves 4 **on the table** *30 mins*
nutritional count per serving *11g total fat (5.4g saturated fat); 828kJ (198 cal); 3.4g carbohydrate; 20.8g protein; 1.3g fibre*

chilli pork and lemon grass parcels

Stir-fry 600g pork mince and 1 finely chopped lemon grass stalk in heated oiled wok until cooked. Add 2 tablespoons thai chilli jam, 2 tablespoons light soy sauce and ⅓ cup coarsely chopped fresh coriander; stir-fry until heated through. Divide pork mixture among four iceberg lettuce leaves; accompany with lime wedges, if you like.

serves 4 **on the table** *15 mins*
nutritional count per serving *10.5g total fat (3.9g saturated fat); 1087kJ (260 cal); 9.5g carbohydrate; 31.1g protein; 1g fibre*

serves 4 on the table 35 mins

8 thick beef sausages (1.2kg)
2 x 400g cans diced tomatoes
200g drained marinated antipasto vegetables
400g can cannellini beans, rinsed, drained
½ cup loosely packed fresh baby basil leaves

italian braised sausages with beans

1 Cook sausages in heated oiled large saucepan until browned. Remove from pan; cut in half lengthways.
2 Add undrained tomatoes and ⅓ cup (80ml) water to same pan; bring to the boil. Return sausages to pan with antipasto vegetables; simmer, covered, 15 minutes.
3 Add beans to pan; simmer, uncovered, about 10 minutes or until thickened slightly.
4 Remove from heat, stir in half the basil; serve topped with remaining basil.
nutritional count per serving *78.1g total fat (36.9g saturated fat); 4113kJ (983 cal); 23g carbohydrate; 41.9g protein; 16g fibre*

We used semi-dried tomatoes, marinated artichokes, grilled eggplant and red capsicum for the antipasto mix; however, any combination of vegetables can be used.

lamb skewers
with chilli jam

Soak bamboo skewers in cold water for at least an hour before using to prevent them from splintering and scorching during cooking.

800g lamb backstrap, cut into 3cm pieces
24 fresh bay leaves
chilli jam
⅓ cup (80ml) sweet chilli sauce
1 tablespoon brown sugar
1 tablespoon lemon juice
1 clove garlic, crushed

1 Thread lamb and bay leaves equally onto eight bamboo skewers. Cook skewers on heated oiled grill plate (or grill or barbecue) until cooked through.
2 Meanwhile, make chilli jam. Serve skewers with jam and mixed salad leaves, if you like.
chilli jam Combine ingredients in small saucepan; stir over low heat until sugar dissolves. Bring to the boil; reduce heat. Simmer, uncovered, about 5 minutes or until jam has thickened slightly.
nutritional count per serving 7.8g total fat (3.3g saturated fat); 1116kJ (267 cal); 7.3g carbohydrate; 41.3g protein; 1g fibre

serves 4 on the table 25 mins

steak sandwich

4 x 125g beef scotch fillet steaks
440ml can stout
2 medium brown onions (300g),
    cut into thin rings
40g baby spinach leaves
2 large tomatoes (440g), sliced thinly
8 thick slices bread (320g), toasted

1 Combine steaks and stout in large shallow dish;
stand 10 minutes.
2 Drain steaks; reserve ½ cup liquid. Cook steaks
in heated oiled large frying pan. Remove from pan;
cover to keep warm.
3 Add onion to same pan; cook, stirring, about
5 minutes or until browned. Add reserved liquid;
bring to the boil. Cook, stirring, about 3 minutes
or until liquid has reduced slightly.
4 Sandwich steak, onion, spinach and tomato
between toast.
nutritional count per serving 10.1g total fat
(3.7g saturated fat); 2157kJ (516 cal);
54.6g carbohydrate; 37.6g protein; 5.1g fibre

Stout is a beer characterised by its dark colour
and strong taste.
We used sourdough bread in this recipe.

paprika lamb wraps

600g lamb backstraps
2 teaspoons sweet smoked paprika
8 large (20cm) flour tortillas (300g)
80g baby rocket leaves
1 cup (150g) drained semi-dried tomatoes in oil
⅓ cup (80ml) sour cream

1 Sprinkle lamb with paprika; cook on heated oiled grill plate (or grill or barbecue) until cooked. Cover lamb; stand 5 minutes then slice thinly.
2 Meanwhile, warm tortillas according to packet directions.
3 Divide rocket and lamb among tortillas; serve with tomatoes and sour cream. Roll wraps to enclose filling.

nutritional count per serving 18.4g total fat (8.2g saturated fat); 2190kJ (524 cal); 44.8g carbohydrate; 40.1g protein; 9.5g fibre

serves 4 on the table 20 mins

veal with lemon
and oregano

¼ cup (80ml) olive oil
2 cloves garlic, sliced thinly
¼ cup fresh oregano leaves
8 x 100g veal escalopes
1 teaspoon lemon rind
⅔ cup (160ml) lemon juice
2 teaspoons finely chopped fresh
    flat-leaf parsley

1 Heat half the oil in large frying pan; cook garlic and oregano, stirring, until garlic is browned lightly and oregano is crisp. Remove with a slotted spoon; drain on absorbent paper.
2 Add remaining oil to pan; cook veal, in batches, until browned both sides. Add rind, juice and parsley to pan; cook 1 minute.
3 Serve veal drizzled with pan juices; sprinkle with garlic and oregano mixture. Serve with mixed salad leaves, if you like.
nutritional count per serving 21.3g total fat (3.4g saturated fat); 1576kJ (377 cal); 1.3g carbohydrate; 45g protein; 0.4g fibre

150g roasted red capsicum in oil
1 cup (70g) stale breadcrumbs
2 tablespoons (45g) basil pesto
40g rocket leaves, chopped coarsely
¼ cup (20g) finely grated parmesan cheese
2 x 350g mini lamb roasts

mini lamb roasts

1 Preheat oven to 200°C/180°C fan-forced.
2 Drain oil from capsicum; reserve 2 tablespoons. Chop capsicum coarsely.
3 Heat reserved oil in medium frying pan; cook breadcrumbs, stirring, until browned lightly. Add pesto, rocket and capsicum; cook, stirring, until rocket wilts. Cool 5 minutes; stir in cheese.
4 Cut a horizontal slit in each roast to make a large pocket, but do not cut all the way through. Press half the bread mixture into each pocket; secure with toothpicks.
5 Heat oiled small baking dish over high heat. Cook lamb, turning, until browned all over. Transfer dish to oven, roast lamb, uncovered, about 20 minutes or until cooked through.
6 Serve lamb with mixed salad leaves, if you like.
nutritional count per serving *32.9g total fat (10.4g saturated fat); 2165kJ (518 cal); 12.8g carbohydrate; 42.5g protein; 1.1g fibre*

serves 4 on the table 20 mins

beef and black bean stir-fry

2 tablespoons peanut oil
700g beef strips
1 large brown onion (200g), sliced thinly
1 large red capsicum (350g), sliced thinly
1 bunch baby choy sum (250g), chopped coarsely
½ cup (125ml) black bean garlic sauce

1 Heat half the oil in wok; stir-fry beef, in batches, until browned.
2 Heat remaining oil in wok; stir-fry onion until soft. Add capsicum to pan; stir-fry 1 minute.
3 Return beef to wok with remaining ingredients and 2 tablespoons water; stir-fry until choy sum wilts. Serve with rice, if you like.
nutritional count per serving *20.9g total fat (6.3g saturated fat); 1739kJ (416 cal); 14.1g carbohydrate; 41.3g protein; 3.3g fibre*

mexican pork cutlets
with chilli corn

4 corn cobs (1.6kg), husks on
50g butter, softened
2 fresh long red chillies, chopped finely
4 x 235g pork cutlets
1 tablespoon vegetable oil
35g packet taco seasoning mix

1   Microwave corn, in husks, on HIGH (100%) about
8 minutes. When cool enough to handle, peel back
husks; remove silk.
2   Combine butter and chilli in small bowl. Drop
spoonfuls of butter onto corn; wrap and tie husks
around corn to enclose. Cook corn on grill plate
(or grill or barbecue) until tender.
3   Meanwhile, rub cutlets with oil then seasoning
mix. Cook pork on grill alongside corn.
4   Remove corn husks, cut each cob into five
pieces. Serve pork with corn, and baby rocket
leaves, if you like.
nutritional count per serving *35.1g total fat*
(13.3g saturated fat); 2976kJ (712cal);
51.5g carbohydrate; 40.8g protein; 14g fibre

serves 4 on the table 35 mins

char siu pork with
spicy fried noodles

600g pork fillets
½ cup (125ml) char siu sauce
450g fresh wide rice noodles
2 tablespoons peanut oil
350g broccolini, chopped coarsely
2 fresh long red chillies, sliced thinly

1 Combine pork and ⅓ cup of the sauce in medium bowl; refrigerate 10 minutes.
2 Cook pork on heated oiled grill plate (or grill or barbecue) until cooked through.
3 Meanwhile, place noodles in large heatproof bowl, cover with boiling water; separate with fork, drain.
4 Heat oil in wok; stir-fry broccolini and chilli until tender. Add noodles, remaining sauce and about a tablespoon of water to wok; stir-fry until hot.
5 Slice pork; serve with noodle mixture.
nutritional count per serving *15.1g total fat (3.1g saturated fat); 1927kJ (461 cal); 37.2g carbohydrate; 38.8g protein; 7.7g fibre*

ginger-chilli pork
with pears

4 x 300g pork loin chops
2 small pears (360g), unpeeled, halved
1 medium red onion (170g), cut into thin wedges
½ cup (125ml) sweet chilli sauce
2cm piece fresh ginger (10g), grated
2 tablespoons lemon juice

1 Cook pork in heated oiled large frying pan; remove from pan, cover to keep warm.
2 Cook pear halves then onion in same pan until browned. Add sauce, ginger and juice to pan; simmer 2 minutes.
3 Serve pork with pear and onion mixture; drizzle with sauce. Serve with mixed salad leaves, if you like.
nutritional count per serving *22g total fat (7.3g saturated fat); 1806kJ (432 cal); 19.8g carbohydrate; 36.9g protein; 4.1g fibre*

serves 4 on the table 20 mins

chicken

thai chicken burgers

Store-bought thai chilli jam can be very hot; use sweet chilli sauce, if you prefer.

500g chicken mince
1 egg
¼ cup finely chopped thai basil leaves
40g baby asian greens
2 tablespoons thai chilli jam
4 ciabatta rolls (460g), split, toasted

1 Combine chicken, egg and basil in medium bowl; shape into four patties.
2 Cook patties in heated oiled large frying pan until cooked through.
3 Sandwich patties, greens and chilli jam between bun halves.
nutritional count per serving *14.7g total fat (3.9g saturated fat); 2094kJ (501 cal); 53.7g carbohydrate; 35.6g protein; 4.1g fibre*

sumac chicken and zucchini skewers

Combine 800g coarsely chopped chicken tenderloins and 2 tablespoons sumac in medium bowl. Halve 2 large zucchini lengthways; chop coarsely. Thread chicken and zucchini onto 12 bamboo skewers; cook on heated oiled grill plate (or grill or barbecue) until chicken is cooked and zucchini is tender. Meanwhile, combine ¾ cup yogurt, 1 tablespoon finely chopped fresh mint and 2 teaspoons lime juice in small bowl. Serve skewers with mint yogurt.

serves 4 on the table *25 mins*
nutritional count per serving *13g total fat (4.5g saturated fat); 1342kJ (321 cal); 3.9g carbohydrate; 46.3g protein; 1.6g fibre*

honey, macadamia chicken stir-fry

Heat 1 tablespoon peanut oil in wok; stir-fry 800g thinly sliced chicken breast fillets until browned, remove from wok. Heat another 1 tablespoon peanut oil in wok; stir-fry 300g coarsely chopped gai lan until tender. Return chicken to wok with ¼ cup japanese soy sauce and 2 tablespoons honey; stir-fry until hot. Serve stir-fry sprinkled with ⅓ cup coarsely chopped roasted macadamias.

serves 4 on the table *25 mins*
nutritional count per serving *29.1g total fat (6.2g saturated fat); 2086kJ (499 cal); 13.4g carbohydrate; 45.4g protein; 1.7g fibre*

chicken and risoni soup

Bring 4 cups chicken stock, 3 cups water and ½ cup dry white wine to the boil in large saucepan; add 400g chicken breast fillets. Reduce heat; simmer, covered, about 10 minutes or until chicken is cooked. Remove chicken from stock mixture; reserve stock mixture. Shred chicken coarsely. Add ⅔ cup risoni to stock mixture; boil until tender. Return chicken to pan with 2 tablespoons lemon juice. Serve soup sprinkled with 2 tablespoons chopped fresh flat-leaf parsley.

serves *4* **on the table** *30 mins*

nutritional count per serving *6.8g total fat (2.3g saturated fat); 1112kJ (266 cal); 18.4g carbohydrate; 27g protein; 0.9g fibre*

mexican chicken pizza

Preheat oven to 220°C/200°C fan-forced. Combine 600g coarsely chopped chicken tenderloins and 35g packet taco seasoning mix in medium bowl. Cook chicken in heated oiled large frying pan. Place eight 60g pizza bases on oven trays; spread with 300g jar chunky tomato salsa. Top pizzas with chicken; sprinkle over 2 cups pizza cheese. Cook 15 minutes or until cheese is browned lightly. Serve pizzas topped with thinly sliced avocado and, if you like, some baby rocket leaves.

makes *8* **on the table** *30 mins*

nutritional count per pizza *17.1g total fat (6.6g saturated fat); 1797kJ (430 cal); 36g carbohydrate; 31.1g protein; 3.5g fibre*

serves 4 on the table 35 mins

2 teaspoons sichuan peppercorns
¼ cup (35g) plain flour
4 chicken thigh cutlets (800g)
400g baby carrots, trimmed, peeled
2 tablespoons tamarind concentrate
1 tablespoon brown sugar

sichuan pepper chicken

1 Preheat oven to 220°C/200°C fan-forced.
2 Using mortar and pestle, finely crush peppercorns. Combine peppercorns and flour in medium bowl, add chicken; toss to coat chicken in mixture, shake off excess.
3 Cook chicken in heated oiled large baking dish until browned all over.
4 Meanwhile, combine carrots, tamarind and sugar in medium bowl. Place carrots around chicken in baking dish; roast, uncovered, in oven, about 20 minutes or until chicken is cooked through. Good served with baby spinach leaves.
nutritional count per serving *20.2g total fat (6.6g saturated fat); 1455kJ (348 cal); 15g carbohydrate; 25g protein; 3.9g fibre*

serves 4 on the table 35 mins

chicken and spinach
cannelloni

1½ cups (240g) shredded barbecued chicken
250g frozen spinach, thawed, chopped coarsely
200g ricotta cheese
12 cannelloni tubes (125g)
700g bottled tomato pasta sauce
¾ cup (75g) coarsely grated pizza cheese

1 Preheat oven to 220°C/200°C fan-forced.
2 Combine chicken, spinach and ricotta in medium bowl; spoon mixture into cannelloni tubes.
3 Spread half the pasta sauce into four small shallow ovenproof dishes; place cannelloni, in single layer, on top of sauce. Pour remaining sauce over cannelloni; sprinkle with pizza cheese.
4 Cover cannelloni with foil; cook about 25 minutes or until pasta is tender.
nutritional count per serving *16g total fat (7.8g saturated fat); 1848kJ (442 cal); 38.6g carbohydrate; 32.4g protein; 5.7g fibre*

You will need to buy half a large (450g) barbecued chicken for this recipe.

red curry chicken
with sugar snap peas

1 tablespoon vegetable oil
800g chicken thigh fillets, chopped coarsely
2 tablespoons red curry paste
400ml can coconut cream
150g sugar snap peas, trimmed
⅓ cup firmly packed fresh coriander leaves

1 Heat half the oil in large saucepan; cook chicken, in batches, until browned.
2 Heat remaining oil in same pan; cook paste, stirring, about 3 minutes or until fragrant.
3 Return chicken to pan with coconut cream; bring to the boil. Reduce heat; simmer, uncovered, 10 minutes or until chicken is cooked through.
4 Add peas to pan; simmer, uncovered, 1 minute or until tender.
5 Serve curry sprinkled with coriander. Accompany with steamed jasmine rice, if you like.

nutritional count per serving 43.4g total fat (23.5g saturated fat); 2433kJ (582 cal); 6.5g carbohydrate; 41g protein; 3g fibre

Red curry paste is available in various strengths in many supermarkets; adjust the amount to suit your palate.

chicken, pumpkin and fetta pizza

You will need to buy half a large (450g) barbecued chicken for this recipe.

400g pumpkin, cut into 1cm pieces
⅓ cup (90g) tomato paste
2 x 170g pizza bases
1½ cups (240g) shredded barbecued chicken
1 small red onion (100g), sliced thinly
200g fetta cheese, crumbled

1 Preheat oven to 220°C/200°C fan-forced.
2 Place pumpkin on oiled oven tray; roast, uncovered, about 10 minutes or until almost tender.
3 Meanwhile, spread paste evenly over pizza bases. Place bases on oven trays; top with pumpkin, chicken, onion and cheese. Bake about 15 minutes or until browned. Serve pizzas sprinkled with fresh mint leaves, if you like.

nutritional count per serving *19.9g total fat (9.6g saturated fat); 2274kJ (544 cal); 54.1g carbohydrate; 34g protein; 5.4g fibre*

serves 4 on the table 30 mins

grilled lemon chicken with crushed potatoes

1kg baby new potatoes
½ cup (125ml) cream
½ cup coarsely chopped fresh flat-leaf parsley
1 teaspoon finely grated lemon rind
1 clove garlic, crushed
12 chicken tenderloins (900g)

1 Boil, steam or microwave potatoes until tender; drain. Mash half the potatoes with cream until almost smooth. Coarsely crush remaining potatoes with the back of a fork until skins burst; fold into mashed potatoes with parsley.

2 Meanwhile, combine rind, garlic and chicken in medium bowl. Cook chicken on heated oiled grill plate (or grill or barbecue) until cooked through. Serve chicken with parsley potatoes; accompany with lemon wedges. Drizzle with a little extra olive oil, if you like.

nutritional count per serving 26.2g total fat (12.2g saturated fat); 2516kJ (602 cal); 33.8g carbohydrate; 54.9g protein; 5.5g fibre

gorgonzola and sage-stuffed chicken

⅓ **cup (50g) semi-dried tomatoes in oil**
4 chicken breast fillets (800g)
100g gorgonzola cheese, cut into four even slices
12 fresh sage leaves
8 slices pancetta (120g)
80g baby rocket leaves

1 Drain tomatoes; reserve 2 tablespoons of the oil.
2 Cut horizontal slits into chicken fillets, three-quarters of the way through, to make pockets.
3 Divide cheese, sage and tomatoes among pockets in chicken. Wrap two pancetta slices around each chicken breast; cook chicken in heated oiled large frying pan until cooked through. Slice chicken thickly.
4 Toss rocket with reserved oil; serve with chicken.
nutritional count per serving *24.3g total fat (10.3g saturated fat); 1940kJ (464 cal); 4.8g carbohydrate; 55.5g protein; 2.1g fibre*

serves 4 on the table 35 mins

1 egg
1 tablespoon dark soy sauce
½ cup (70g) finely chopped roasted peanuts
½ cup (50g) packaged breadcrumbs
¼ cup finely chopped fresh coriander
20 chicken drumettes (1.4kg)

peanut and coriander crumbed drumettes

1 Preheat oven to 220°C/200°C fan-forced.
2 Whisk egg and sauce in small shallow bowl. Combine nuts, breadcrumbs and coriander in another small shallow bowl. Dip chicken in egg mixture, then in crumb mixture to coat.
3 Place chicken on oiled wire rack over large baking dish. Roast chicken, uncovered, about 25 minutes or until cooked through.
4 Serve chicken with mixed salad leaves and sweet chilli sauce, if you like.
nutritional count per serving *31g total fat (7.8g saturated fat); 2090kJ (488 cal); 10g carbohydrate; 41.6g protein; 2g fibre*
Use granulated or crushed peanuts to save time.

serves 4 on the table 30 mins

five-spice chicken with mushroom sauce

4 chicken breast fillets (800g)
2 teaspoons five-spice powder
1 tablespoon olive oil
200g fresh shiitake mushrooms, sliced thinly
1 tablespoon japanese soy sauce
270ml can coconut cream

1 Coat chicken with five-spice; cook in heated oiled large frying pan. Remove from pan; cover chicken to keep warm.

2 Add oil and mushrooms to same pan; cook, stirring occasionally, until mushrooms are soft. Add sauce and coconut cream to pan; simmer, uncovered, until sauce thickens slightly.

3 Serve chicken with mushroom sauce and steamed green beans, if you like.

nutritional count per serving *29.6g total fat (16.3g saturated fat); 1944kJ (465 cal); 3.9g carbohydrate; 45.2g protein; 2.3g fibre*
This dish goes well with steamed jasmine rice.

dukkah-crusted chicken and chips

750g packet frozen potato chips
4 x 200g chicken breast fillets
1 egg, beaten lightly
¾ cup (105g) dukkah
⅔ cup (190g) mayonnaise
1 tablespoon sweet chilli sauce

1 Preheat oven to 220°C/200°C fan-forced.
2 Place chips, in single layer, on oiled oven tray; bake about 30 minutes or until crisp.
3 Meanwhile, dip chicken in egg, then in dukkah to coat. Place chicken on oiled wire rack over large baking dish; bake, uncovered, alongside chips, about 20 minutes or until chicken is cooked through.
4 Combine mayonnaise and sauce. Slice chicken thickly, serve with chips and mayonnaise.

nutritional count per serving *51.6g total fat (13.2g saturated fat); 4255kJ (1018 cal); 45.1g carbohydrate; 38g protein; 11.6g fibre*

balsamic chicken with eggplant purée

8 chicken drumsticks (1.2kg)
2 tablespoons balsamic vinegar
2 tablespoons brown sugar
1 large eggplant (500g), halved lengthways
6 medium egg tomatoes (450g), halved
⅓ cup loosely packed fresh baby basil leaves

1 Preheat oven to 240°C/220°C fan-forced.
2 Combine chicken, vinegar and sugar in large shallow baking dish. Cover dish; roast chicken 15 minutes.
3 Meanwhile, pierce eggplant all over with fork; place, cut-side down, on oiled oven tray. Roast, uncovered, about 15 minutes or until tender. When cool enough to handle, peel eggplant; blend or process eggplant until smooth.
4 Uncover chicken; add tomato to dish. Roast, uncovered, about 15 minutes or until chicken is cooked through.
5 Serve chicken with eggplant purée and tomato; drizzle with pan juices then sprinkle with basil. Serve with mixed salad leaves, if you like.
nutritional count per serving *21.4g total fat (6.3g saturated fat); 1643kJ (393 cal); 12.2g carbohydrate; 36g protein; 4.5g fibre*

serves 4 on the table 20 mins

vegetables

corn, pea and
bean stir-fry

4 trimmed corn cobs (1kg)
50g butter
2 cloves garlic, crushed
300g sugar snap peas, trimmed
350g green beans, trimmed

1 Boil, steam or microwave corn until just tender. When cool enough to handle, cut kernels from cobs.
2 Meanwhile, melt butter in large frying pan. Add garlic; cook, stirring, 2 minutes. Add corn, peas and beans; cook until beans are tender.
nutritional count per serving 13.6g total fat (7g saturated fat); 1672kJ (400 cal); 46.9g carbohydrate; 14.8g protein; 15.6g fibre

avocado, bacon and tomato panini

Pan-fry 8 rindless bacon rashers until crisp. Meanwhile, split and toast cut sides of four panini bread rolls; spread with ⅓ cup mayonnaise. Fill rolls with 1 medium thinly sliced avocado, 2 medium thinly sliced tomatoes, 60g mesclun and bacon.

serves 4 on the table *15 mins*
nutritional count per serving *25.8g total fat (6.4g saturated fat); 1731kJ (414 cal); 24g carbohydrate; 20.3g protein; 3.1g fibre*

Use turkish rolls if panini rolls aren't available.

spiced pumpkin and coconut soup

Reserve ½ cup coconut cream from 400ml can coconut cream. Combine remaining coconut cream, 1 medium coarsely chopped brown onion, 500g coarsely chopped pumpkin, 1 small coarsely chopped kumara, 3 cups water and 1 tablespoon curry paste in large saucepan. Bring to the boil; reduce heat, simmer, uncovered, 10 minutes or until vegetables are soft. Blend or process mixture, in batches, until smooth. Meanwhile, heat reserved coconut cream in small saucepan without boiling. Serve soup drizzled with coconut cream.

serves 4 on the table *30 mins*
nutritional count per serving *23.1g total fat (18.7g saturated fat); 1375kJ (329 cal); 21.8g carbohydrate; 6.4g protein; 5.3g fibre*

antipasto ciabatta rolls

Thinly slice 1 medium eggplant, sprinkle slices with 1 tablespoon ground cumin. Cook eggplant, in batches, on heated oiled grill plate. Split and toast cut sides of 4 ciabatta bread rolls; spread rolls with ½ cup hummus, then sandwich eggplant, ⅔ cup drained sun-dried tomatoes and 40g baby rocket leaves among rolls.

serves *4* **on the table** *25 mins*
nutritional count per serving *8.3g total fat (1.4g saturated fat); 966kJ (231 cal); 25.9g carbohydrate; 8.9g protein; 8.4g fibre*

pea and bacon soup

Combine 1 coarsely chopped leek, 500g frozen baby peas, 3 cups vegetable stock and 300ml cream in large saucepan. Bring to the boil; reduce heat, simmer, uncovered, 10 minutes or until vegetables are soft. Blend or process mixture, in batches, until smooth. Meanwhile, finely chop 2 rindless bacon rashers; pan-fry until crisp. Sprinkle soup with bacon; serve with grissini sticks, if you like.

serves *4* **on the table** *20 mins*
nutritional count per serving *36.9g total fat (22.8g saturated fat); 1881kJ (450 cal); 12.3g carbohydrate; 15.3g protein; 8.4g fibre*

serves 4 on the table 25 mins

mushroom stroganoff

1½ cups (300g) white long-grain rice
700g button mushrooms, sliced thickly
40g packet beef stroganoff recipe base
1 large red capsicum (350g), sliced thinly
2 tablespoons sour cream
3 green onions, sliced thinly

1 Cook rice in large saucepan of boiling water, uncovered, until tender; drain.

2 Meanwhile, cook mushrooms in heated oiled large frying pan until almost tender. Add stroganoff base, 1¼ cups (310ml) water and capsicum; cook, stirring, until capsicum is tender. Remove from heat; stir in sour cream and half the onions. Serve with rice and remaining onions.

nutritional count per serving 5.5g total fat (2.8g saturated fat); 1626kJ (389 cal); 67.3g carbohydrate; 13.4g protein; 7g fibre

1 medium eggplant (300g), chopped coarsely
1 large red capsicum (350g), chopped coarsely
400g can diced tomatoes
¼ cup loosely packed fresh baby basil leaves
cheesy polenta
1 cup (170g) polenta
1 cup (80g) finely grated parmesan cheese

cheesy polenta
with ratatouille

1 Cook eggplant and capsicum in heated oiled large frying pan until tender. Add undrained tomatoes; simmer, uncovered, 5 minutes or until mixture thickens slightly.

2 Meanwhile, make cheesy polenta.

3 Serve polenta with ratatouille; sprinkle with basil.

cheesy polenta Bring 1.25 litres (4½ cups) water to the boil in large saucepan; gradually stir in polenta. Reduce heat; cook, stirring, about 10 minutes or until polenta thickens. Remove from heat; stir in cheese. Stand 3 minutes before serving.

nutritional count per serving 7.9g total fat (4.2g saturated fat); 1208kJ (289 cal); 37.5g carbohydrate; 14g protein; 5.3g fibre

makes 12 on the table 35 mins

spinach pies

1 tablespoon olive oil
1 large brown onion (200g), chopped finely
375g baby spinach leaves
1 teaspoon lemon rind
¼ cup (60ml) lemon juice
3 sheets ready-rolled puff pastry
2 tablespoons pine nuts

1   Preheat oven to 220°C/200°C fan-forced. Line oven tray with baking paper.
2   Heat oil in large frying pan; cook onion, stirring, until softened. Add half the spinach; cook, stirring, until wilted. Add remaining spinach, rind and juice to pan; cook, stirring, until liquid has evaporated. Remove from heat, cool 5 minutes.
3   Using 11cm-round cutter, cut 12 rounds from pastry. Divide spinach mixture among rounds. Gather three points of each round together to form a triangle, leaving top of filling exposed. Pinch and twist each corner to secure pasty round. Place pies on oven tray.
4   Sprinkle filling with pine nuts. Bake pies about 15 minutes or until pastry is browned. Good served with lemon yogurt.
nutritional count per pie *11.1g total fat (5.3g saturated fat); 757kJ (181 cal); 16.3g carbohydrate; 3.4g protein; 1.6g fibre*

bean nachos

420g can kidney beans, rinsed, drained
300g jar thick and chunky tomato salsa
230g packet cheese-flavoured corn chips
2 cups (240g) coarsely grated cheddar cheese
1 small avocado (200g), mashed
⅔ cup (160g) sour cream

1   Preheat oven to 200°C/180°C fan-forced.
2   Combine beans, salsa and ½ cup (125ml) water in medium frying pan; bring to the boil. Reduce heat, simmer, uncovered, about 8 minutes or until mixture is thickened slightly.
3   Meanwhile, place corn chips in four ovenproof dishes; sprinkle with cheese. Place dishes on oven tray. Bake, in oven, about 5 minutes or until cheese has melted.
4   Top hot corn chips with bean mixture and avocado. Serve with sour cream.

nutritional count per serving *61.3g total fat (31.8g saturated fat); 3595kJ (860 cal); 46.2 g carbohydrate; 26.5g protein; 12.1g fibre*

serves 4 on the table 35 mins

1 cup coarsely chopped pumpkin (160g)
300g packet instant mash
½ cup (125ml) buttermilk
125g can corn kernels, rinsed, drained
½ cup coarsely chopped fresh flat-leaf parsley
½ cup (75g) sesame seeds, toasted

pumpkin and
corn patties

1 Boil, steam or microwave pumpkin until tender; drain.
2 Combine instant mash, 3 cups (750ml) boiling water and buttermilk in large heatproof bowl. Stir in pumpkin, corn and parsley; stand 5 minutes.
3 Shape mixture into eight patties; coat with sesame seeds.
4 Cook patties, in batches, in heated oiled large frying pan, until heated through. Good served with baby rocket leaves.
nutritional count per serving *15.8g total fat (4.2g saturated fat); 1831kJ (438 cal); 56.5g carbohydrate; 12.5g protein; 9.7g fibre*

Instant mash is a dried mashed potato mix reconstituted with boiling liquid to give a light buttery flavour. It is available from most supermarkets.
Toast sesame seeds in a small frying pan, over medium heat, shaking pan occasionally, until golden and fragrant, about 3-5 minutes.

300ml thickened cream
1 tablespoon icing sugar
2 x 18cm-round bought sponge cakes (460g)
¼ cup (60ml) melon-flavoured liqueur
300g rockmelon, chopped coarsely
300g honeydew melon, chopped coarsely

desserts

melon tiramisu

We used Midori in this recipe, a honeydew melon-flavoured liqueur.
If you have the time, this dessert is best made a day ahead and refrigerated, covered, overnight.

1 Beat cream and sifted icing sugar in small bowl with electric mixer until soft peaks form.
2 Split cakes in half horizontally; trim brown edges. Cut 12 x 6.5cm rounds from cakes. Place one cake round in each of six 1½ cup (375ml) glasses; drizzle with half the liqueur.
3 Divide half the combined melons and cream over cake. Repeat layering with remaining cake, liqueur, and melon mixture.
nutritional count per serving *22.2g total fat (15.2g saturated fat); 2006kJ (480 cal); 57.5g carbohydrate; 7.8g protein; 1.8g fibre*

coffee hazelnut shots

Combine ⅓ cup hazelnut-flavoured liqueur, ¼ cup water, 2 tablespoons instant coffee granules and 2 tablespoons brown sugar in small saucepan; stir, over low heat, until sugar dissolves. Boil about 5 minutes or until syrup thickens slightly. Divide 500ml hazelnut gelato among four serving glasses; pour over coffee syrup. Serve sprinkled with ¼ cup coarsely chopped roasted hazelnuts.
serves 4 on the table *20 mins*
nutritional count per serving *5.5g total fat (0.3g saturated fat); 1229kJ (294 cal); 48.3g carbohydrate; 3.4g protein; 4.5g fibre*

ice-cream fondue

Place 100g melted milk chocolate, ⅓ cup toasted shredded coconut, ⅓ cup finely chopped peanut brittle, ⅓ cup finely chopped peppermint crisp and 2 tablespoons hundreds and thousands in six separate small bowls. Serve with six 50g mini choc-coated vanilla ice-creams on sticks, for dipping.
serves 6 on the table *10 mins*
nutritional count per serving *16.1g total fat (10.8g saturated fat); 1287kJ (308 cal); 36.4g carbohydrate; 4g protein; 0.9g fibre*

crêpes with ice-cream and passionfruit sauce

To make passionfruit sauce, warm ¾ cup cream in small saucepan over low heat; remove from heat, stir in ½ cup passionfruit pulp. Heat 400g packet frozen crêpes according to directions on the packet. Serve crêpes with sauce and two scoops of ice-cream.
serves *4* on the table *10 mins*
nutritional count per serving *31.3g total fat (19.3g saturated fat); 1990kJ (476 cal); 36g carbohydrate; 10.6g protein; 5.3g fibre*

raspberry coconut cream

Whip 300ml thickened cream and 2 tablespoons sifted icing sugar in small bowl with electric mixer until soft peaks form; transfer to medium bowl. Fold in ⅔ cup thick vanilla custard and 100g crumbled coconut macaroons. Layer into serving glasses with 125g raspberries; top with crumbled chocolate flake.
serves *6* on the table *15 mins*
nutritional count per serving *28.3g total fat (18.8g saturated fat); 1526kJ (365 cal); 23.6g carbohydrate; 3.5g protein; 2.6g fibre*

serves 4 on the table 35 mins

blackberry ice-cream sandwiches

2 cups (300g) frozen blackberries, thawed
500ml ice-cream, softened
12 bought brandy snaps (150g)

1 Fold drained berries into ice-cream.
2 Working quickly, place half the brandy snaps on baking-paper-lined tray; place a scoop of ice-cream on top of each brandy snap, then top with remaining biscuits; press down gently. Freeze 20 minutes before serving.
nutritional count per serving *16g total fat (9.6g saturated fat); 1467kJ (351 cal); 48.5g carbohydrate; 5.7g protein; 5.3g fibre*

1 sheet ready-rolled shortcrust pastry
½ cup (150g) fruit mince
1 medium apple (150g), peeled, cored,
  sliced thinly
1 egg
2 teaspoons white sugar
½ teaspoon mixed spice

spiced apple and
fruit mince tarts

Fruit mince is a mixture of dried fruits such as raisins, sultanas and candied peel, nuts, spices, apple, brandy or rum. It is used as a filling for cakes, puddings and fruit mince pies.

1 Preheat oven to 200°C/180°C fan-forced. Line oven tray with baking paper.
2 Cut pastry sheet into quarters. Fold 1cm border around each pastry square; press firmly. Place pastry on oven tray.
3 Spread fruit mince in centre of each square; top with apple. Brush apples with egg; sprinkle with combined sugar and spice.
4 Bake about 20 minutes. Serve with custard, if you like.
nutritional count per serve 14g total fat (6.8g saturated fat); 1346kJ (322 cal); 42.7g carbohydrate; 4.9g protein; 2.5g fibre

makes 12 on the table 25 mins

lemon meringue tarts

12 (275g) small frozen sweet tart cases
340g jar lemon curd
3 egg whites
¾ cup (165g) caster sugar

1 Preheat oven to 180°C/160°C fan-forced.
2 Place tart cases on oven tray; bake cases
10 minutes, cool. Increase oven temperature
to 240°C/220°C fan-forced.
3 Fill tart cases with lemon curd.
4 Beat egg whites in small bowl with electric mixer
until soft peaks form; gradually add sugar, beating
until dissolved between additions. Pipe or spoon
meringue over lemon curd.
5 Return tarts to oven; bake about 5 minutes or
until meringue is browned lightly.
nutritional count per serving *14g total fat*
(6.2g saturated fat); 1254kJ (300 cal);
40.3g carbohydrate; 4g protein; 0.6g fibre

strawberry shortcakes

2 sheets ready-rolled shortcrust pastry
250g strawberries, quartered
1 tablespoon orange-flavoured liqueur
⅓ cup (110g) strawberry jam
¾ cup (180ml) thickened cream, whipped
1 tablespoon icing sugar

1 Preheat oven to 200°C/180°C fan-forced. Line oven trays with baking paper.
2 Using 8cm-round fluted cutter, cut 12 rounds from pastry; place on trays. Bake rounds about 10 minutes or until crisp; cool.
3 Meanwhile, combine strawberries and liqueur in small bowl.
4 Spread jam over eight pastry rounds; place four on serving plates. Top shortcakes with half the strawberries and cream, then another shortcake; repeat with remaining strawberries and cream, then top with remaining shortcake. Dust with sifted icing sugar.
nutritional count per serving *39.7g total fat (23.1g saturated fat); 2721kJ (651 cal); 63.2g carbohydrate; 7.4g protein; 3.3g fibre*

makes 4 on the table 30 mins

soft-centred
choc-mint cakes

A mint pattie is a round chocolate-coated confectionery with a soft peppermint centre. It is available from most supermarkets.

100g coarsely chopped dark eating chocolate
90g butter, chopped
3 eggs, separated
2 tablespoons caster sugar
2 tablespoons plain flour
2 x 20g mint patties

1 Preheat oven to 180°C/160°C fan-forced. Grease four holes of 6-hole (¾-cup/180ml) texas muffin pan.
2 Stir chocolate and butter in small saucepan over low heat until smooth; cool 5 minutes.
3 Meanwhile, beat egg yolks and sugar in small bowl, until thick and creamy; stir in sifted flour and chocolate mixture.
4 Beat egg whites, in clean small bowl, until soft peaks form; fold into chocolate mixture. Spoon mixture into pan holes; bake 5 minutes.
5 Cut mint patties into quarters; push 2 quarters into centre of each cake. Bake cakes 6 minutes.
6 Stand cakes 2 minutes before serving warm. Dust with sifted cocoa, if you like.
nutritional count per serving *28.5g total fat (18.3g saturated fat); 1768kJ (423 cal); 34.8g carbohydrate; 7g protein; 0.6g fibre*

serves 4 on the table 30 mins

white chocolate pancakes with mango

1 cup (150g) self-raising flour
¼ cup (55g) caster sugar
2 eggs
1 cup (250ml) buttermilk
1 cup (190g) white Choc Bits
300g frozen mango cheeks, thawed
1 tablespoon caster sugar, extra

1 Sift flour and sugar into medium bowl; gradually whisk in combined eggs and buttermilk until smooth. Add Choc Bits to batter; stir until combined.
2 Heat greased small frying pan, pour in ¼ cup batter; cook pancake until browned both sides. Repeat with remaining batter.
3 Meanwhile, blend or process mango and extra sugar until smooth. Place purée in heated small saucepan; stir until warmed through.
4 Serve pancakes drizzled with mango purée, and whipped cream, if you like.
nutritional count per serving *19.7g total fat (10.4g saturated fat); 2437kJ (583 cal); 85.5g carbohydrate; 13.8g protein; 2.6g fibre*

choc-peanut banana turnovers

1 medium banana (200g), chopped finely
½ cup (140g) crunchy peanut butter
100g dark eating chocolate, chopped coarsely
3 sheets ready-rolled puff pastry
1 egg, beaten lightly
2 tablespoons white sugar

1 Preheat oven to 200°C/180°C fan-forced. Line oven tray with baking paper.
2 Combine banana, peanut butter and chocolate in medium bowl.
3 Using 10cm-round cutter, cut 12 rounds from pastry; place 1 level tablespoon banana mixture in centre of each round. Brush pastry edges with a little egg; fold in half to enclose filling, pinch edges to seal.
4 Place pastries on tray; brush with remaining egg, sprinkle with sugar. Bake about 20 minutes.

nutritional count per turnover *18.2g total fat (7.6g saturated fat); 1241kJ (297 cal); 25.8g carbohydrate; 6.7g protein; 2.2g fibre*

makes 8 on the table 35 mins

chocolate fig brownies

560g packet brownie mix
4 fresh figs, halved

1 Preheat oven to 200°C/180°C fan-forced. Line 19cm x 29cm slice pan with baking paper.
2 Make brownie mix according to directions on packet. Pour into pan; bake 10 minutes.
3 Place fig halves, cut-side up, over brownie mixture. Bake 20 minutes. Cool in pan; when cold, cut brownie in eight pieces.
nutritional count per serving *10.1g total fat (1.8g saturated fat); 907kJ (217 cal); 28g carbohydrate; 2.8g protein; 1.3g fibre*

serves 4 on the table 30 mins

white chocolate and
raspberry french toast

3 thick slices (195g) white bread
130g coarsely chopped white eating chocolate
125g raspberries
2 eggs
⅓ cup (80ml) milk
30g butter

1 Cut slits horizontally into bread slices three-quarters of the way through to make pockets. Divide chocolate and raspberries between pockets.

2 Dip pockets into combined egg and milk. Melt 10g butter in large frying pan; cook one bread slice until browned both sides. Repeat with remaining bread, using 10g butter for each slice.

3 Cut toasts into quarters; serve hot, with cream and extra fresh raspberries and dusted with sifted icing sugar, if you like.

nutritional count per serving 21.7g total fat (12.4g saturated fat); 1722kJ (415 cal); 42.6g carbohydrate; 10.8g protein; 3.1g fibre

Buy a high-top unsliced white bread loaf and cut into three 2cm-thick slices.

black forest ice-cream sandwich

415g can seedless black cherries in syrup
¼ cup (55g) caster sugar
4 x 50g vanilla ice-cream slices
4 x 6cm square lamingtons (320g), halved

1   Drain cherries; reserve syrup. Stir syrup and sugar in small saucepan over heat until sugar dissolves. Boil, uncovered, about 5 minutes or until syrup thickens slightly.

2   Sandwich ice-cream slices between lamingtons. Place onto serving plates; top with cherries then drizzle with syrup.

nutritional count per serving 14.9g total fat (11g saturated fat); 2019kJ (483 cal); 78.7g carbohydrate; 6.3g protein; 3.1g fibre

You can trim the ice cream slice to fit the lamington, if you like.

glossary

ASIAN GREENS a packaged mix of baby buk choy, choy sum, gai lan and water spinach. Available from selected supermarkets and greengrocers.

BASIL an aromatic herb; there are many types, but the most commonly used is sweet, or common, basil.
thai also known as horapa; different from holy basil and sweet basil in both look and taste, having smaller leaves and purplish stems. Has a light licorice or aniseed taste, and is one of the basic flavours that typify Thai cuisine.

BEANS
cannellini small white bean similar in appearance and flavour to haricot, navy or great northern beans – all of which can be substituted for each other.
kidney medium-sized red bean, slightly floury in texture yet sweet in flavour; sold dried or canned.
mexe-beans a mexican-style bean mix; mildly-spiced canned combination of kidney or pinto beans, capsicum and tomato.
sprouts also known as bean shoots; tender new growths of assorted beans and seeds germinated for consumption as sprouts. The most readily available are mung bean, soya bean, alfalfa and snow pea sprouts.

BROCCOLINI a cross between broccoli and chinese kale; milder and sweeter than broccoli. Each long stem is topped by a loose floret that closely resembles broccoli; from floret to stem, broccolini is completely edible.

BROWNIE MIX an American chocolate dessert made very much like cake, however, brownies are not leavened with baking powder, so are denser and heavier. They are usually uniced, and are cut into squares or bars to serve. Brownie mix is now available from supermarkets in the cake aisle.

BUK CHOY also known as bok choy, pak choi, chinese white cabbage or chinese chard; has a fresh, mild mustard taste. Use both stems and leaves. Baby buk choy, also known as pak kat farang or shanghai bok choy, is smaller and more tender than buk choy, and has a mildly acrid, distinctive taste.

BUTTER use salted or unsalted (sweet) butter; 125g is equal to 4 ounces (one stick) of butter.

BUTTERMILK originally the term given to the slightly sour liquid left after butter was churned from cream, today it is commercially made similarly to yogurt. Despite the implication of its name, it is low in fat.

CANNELLONI a wide tubular pasta about 7-10cm in length that is filled with meat or cheese.

CAPSICUM also known as bell pepper or, simply, pepper. Membranes and seeds should be discarded before use.

CHEESE
gorgonzola a creamy Italian blue cheese having a mild, sweet taste.
haloumi a firm, cream-coloured sheep milk cheese matured in brine; a bit like a minty, salty fetta in flavour. Haloumi can be grilled or fried, briefly, without breaking down. Should be eaten while still warm as it becomes tough and rubbery on cooling.
mascarpone a cultured cream product made in much the same way as yogurt. It's whitish to creamy yellow in colour, with a soft, creamy texture and a slightly tangy taste.
pecorino the generic Italian name for cheeses made from sheep milk. It's a hard, white to pale yellow cheese. If you can't find it, use parmesan.
pizza a commercial blend of varying proportions of processed grated mozzarella, cheddar and parmesan.

CHICKEN DRUMETTES small fleshy part of the wing between the shoulder and the elbow, trimmed to resemble a drumstick.

CHOCOLATE
choc Bits also known as chocolate chips or chocolate morsels. Hold their shape in baking, and are ideal for decorating.
dark eating also known as semi-sweet or luxury chocolate; made of a high percentage of cocoa liquor and cocoa butter, and little added sugar.
Flake a crumbly chocolate bar consisting of layers of "flaky" chocolate, hence the name.

milk eating the most popular eating chocolate, mild and very sweet; similar in make-up to dark eating chocolate, but with the addition of milk powder.
white eating contains no cocoa solids but derives its sweet flavour from cocoa butter. Very sensitive to heat.

CHORIZO a sausage of Spanish origin, made of coarsely ground pork and highly seasoned with garlic and chillies.

CHOY SUM also known as pakaukeo or flowering cabbage, a member of the buk choy family; easy to identify with its long stems, light green leaves and yellow flowers. Is eaten, stems and all.

CORIANDER also known as pak chee, cilantro or chinese parsley; a green-leafed herb with a pungent flavour. Both the stems and roots of coriander are used in Thai cooking.

CORN CHIPS made from ground corn that is made into a dough, and rolled, toasted and fried until crisp.

CORNFLOUR also known as cornstarch.

COUSCOUS a semolina flour and water dough is sieved then dehydrated to produce minuscule even-sized pellets of couscous; it is rehydrated by steaming or with the addition of a warm liquid and swells to three or four times its original size.

CREAM we use fresh cream unless otherwise stated. Also known as pure or pouring cream.
sour a thick cultured soured cream. Minimum fat content 35%.
thickened a whipping cream containing a thickener. Minimum fat content 35%.

DUKKAH traditionally an Egyptian specialty made of roasted nuts, seeds and aromatic spices. Available from some supermarkets, Middle-Eastern food stores and speciality spice shops.

EGGPLANT also known as aubergine.

FIVE-SPICE POWDER a mixture of ground cinnamon, cloves, star anise, sichuan pepper and fennel seeds. Also known as chinese five-spice.

FLOUR
plain an all-purpose flour made from wheat.

self-raising plain flour sifted with baking powder in the proportion of 1 cup flour to 2 teaspoons baking powder.

GAI LAN also known as gai larn, kanah, gai lum, chinese kale and chinese broccoli; appreciated more for its stems than its coarse leaves.

GARLIC CHIVES also known as chinese chives; have rougher, flatter leaves than simple chives, and a pink-tinged teardrop-shaped flowering bud at the end. Are strongly flavoured.

GINGER also known as green or root ginger; the thick root of a tropical plant.

HAZELNUT-FLAVOURED LIQUEUR we use Frangelico, but you can use your favourite brand.

HUNDREDS AND THOUSANDS nonpareils; tiny sugar-syrup-coated sugar crystals that come in a variety of bright colours and are used to decorate cakes and party foods.

KUMARA Polynesian name of orange-fleshed sweet potato often confused with yam.

LAMB
backstrap the larger fillet from a row of loin chops or cutlets.
mini roasts cut from the lamb leg; has no bone.

LAMINGTONS cubes of sponge, or more traditionally, butter cake, cut into about 5cm (2 inch) squares, then coated in a layer of chocolate icing and covered with desiccated coconut.

LEBANESE CUCUMBER short, slender and thin-skinned. Probably the most popular variety because of its tender, edible skin, tiny, yielding seeds and sweet, fresh and flavoursome taste.

LEMON GRASS a tall, clumping, lemon-smelling and -tasting, sharp-edged grass; the white lower part of each stem is chopped and used in Asian cooking.

MACAROONS, COCONUT a sweet biscuit made of almonds, sugar and egg white.

MELON-FLAVOURED LIQUEUR we used Midori but you can use your favourite brand.

MESCLUN a mixture of young lettuce and other green leaves, including baby spinach, mizuna and curly endive. Also sold as salad mix or gourmet salad mix.

MINCE also known as ground meat.

MINT PATTIE a round-shaped confectionery with a peppermint centre covered in chocolate. It is available from most supermarkets.

MUSHROOMS, SHIITAKE when fresh are also known as chinese black or forest mushrooms; although cultivated, they have the earthiness and taste of wild mushrooms. When dried, they are known as donko or dried chinese mushrooms; rehydrate before use.

NOODLES
fresh rice also known as ho fun, khao pun, sen yau, pho or kway tiau. Can be purchased in strands of various widths or large sheets weighing about 500g that are cut into the desired noodle size. Chewy and pure white, they do not need pre-cooking before use.
singapore pre-cooked wheat noodles best described as a thinner version of hokkien.
soba thin spaghetti-like pale brown noodle made from buckwheat and varying proportions of wheat flour.

NUTS to roast, place shelled, peeled nuts, in single layer, in small dry frying pan; cook, over low heat, until fragrant and just changed in colour. Or spread, in a single layer, on oven tray; roast in moderate oven for 8-10 minutes. Be careful to avoid burning nuts.

ONIONS
green also known as scallion or, incorrectly, shallot. An immature onion picked before the bulb has formed; has a long, bright-green edible stalk.
shallots also called french shallots, golden shallots or eschalots; small, brown-skinned, elongated members of the onion family.
red also known as spanish, red spanish or bermuda onion; a sweet-flavoured, large, purple-red onion.

ORANGE-FLAVOURED LIQUEUR we used Grand Marnier, but you can use your favourite brand.

PANCETTA an Italian unsmoked bacon that is cured but not smoked.

PARSLEY, FLAT-LEAF also known as continental parsley or italian parsley.

PEANUT BRITTLE peanuts covered in a hard toffee coating; available from confectionery and department stores and some major supermarkets.

PEPPERMINT CRISP a confectionery bar with a crisp centre of peppermint that is covered with chocolate.

PERI-PERI SPICE MIX (also piri-piri) contains a blend of hot chilli powder, paprika, cumin, ginger and lemon.

POLENTA also known as cornmeal; a flour-like cereal made of dried corn (maize) sold ground in several textures. Also the name of the dish made from it.

POMEGRANATE a dark-red, leathery-skinned fruit about the size of an orange filled with hundreds of seeds, wrapped in a lucent-crimson pulp and having a tangy sweet-sour flavour.

POTATO
baby new also known as chats; not a separate variety but an early harvest with very thin skin.
instant mash a dried mashed potato mix reconstituted with boiling liquid giving a light buttery flavour.
kipfler small, finger-shaped, knobby potato with a nutty flavour.

PROSCIUTTO cured, air-dried (unsmoked), pressed ham.

RISONI also known as risi; small, rice-shaped pasta very similar to another small pasta, orzo.

ROCKET also known as arugula, rugula and rucola; a peppery-tasting green leaf. Baby rocket (wild rocket) leaves are both smaller and less peppery.

SAUCES
black bean made from fermented soya beans, spices, water and wheat flour.
char siu a Chinese barbecue sauce made from sugar, water, salt, honey, fermented soya bean paste, soy sauce, malt syrup and spices. It can be found at most supermarkets.
pizza tomato commercially made tomato sauce spread over pizza bases.

satay traditional Indonesian/Malaysian spicy peanut and coconut sauce.

soy made from fermented soya beans. Several variations are available in most supermarkets and Asian food stores.

dark soy deep brown, almost black in colour; rich, with a thicker consistency than other types. Pungent but not very salty; it is good for marinating.

japanese soy an all-purpose low-sodium sauce made with more wheat content than its Chinese counterparts. Possibly the best table soy and the one to choose if you only want one variety.

light soy fairly thin in consistency and, while paler than the others, the saltiest tasting; used in dishes in which the natural colour of the ingredients is to be maintained. Not to be confused with salt-reduced or low-sodium sauces.

sweet chilli a comparatively mild, Thai-type sauce made from red chillies, sugar, garlic and vinegar.

teriyaki made from soy sauce, mirin, sugar, ginger and other spices.

tomato pasta made of a blend of tomatoes, herbs and spices.

SAUSAGES also known as snags or bangers. Minced meat is seasoned with salt and spices, mixed with cereal and packed into casings.

SEAFOOD

blue-eye also known as deep sea trevalla or trevally and blue-eye cod; thick, moist white-fleshed fish.

firm white fish fillets any boneless firm white fish fillet – blue-eye, bream, ling, swordfish or whiting are all good choices. Check for any small bones and use tweezers to remove them.

prawns also known as shrimp.

salmon red-pink firm flesh with few bones; has a moist delicate flavour.

snapper a moist, mild, delicate, sweet flavoured fish with a medium textured flesh and easily removed bones.

squid is a type of mollusc; also known as calamari. Buy squid hoods to make preparation easier.

trout, smoked can be found, cryovac-packed, in the refrigerated section of supermarkets and fish shops.

SHALLOTS see onions.

SICHUAN PEPPERCORNS also known as chinese pepper. Small, red-brown aromatic seeds resembling black peppercorns; they have a peppery-lemon flavour.

SKEWERS if using bamboo skewers, soak them in cold water for an hour before using to prevent them splintering and scorching during cooking.

SNOW PEAS also called mange tout (eat all). Snow pea tendrils are the growing shoots of the plant, and snow pea sprouts are the tender new growths of snow peas.

SPINACH also known as english spinach and, incorrectly, silver beet.

STOUT a type of beer characterised by its dark colour and heavily roasted bitter, rich flavour. It is brewed from barley, hops, brewers yeast and water. Guinness is one of the better known stouts on the market.

SUGAR

brown an extremely soft, finely granulated sugar retaining molasses for its characteristic colour and flavour.

caster also known as superfine or finely granulated table sugar.

icing also known as confectioners' sugar or powdered sugar; granulated sugar crushed together with a small amount of added cornflour.

white a coarse, granulated table sugar, also known as crystal sugar.

SUGAR SNAP PEAS also known as honey snap peas; fresh small peas that can be eaten whole, pod and all, similarly to snow peas.

SUMAC a purple-red, astringent spice ground from berries growing on shrubs that flourish wild around the Mediterranean; has a tart, lemony flavour. Found in Middle-Eastern food stores and speciality spice shops.

TAMARIND CONCENTRATE the commercial distillation of tamarind pulp into a condensed paste. Used straight from the container with no soaking or straining required; can be diluted with water according to taste. Found in Asian food stores and most major supermarkets.

TATSOI also known as rosette buk choy; is a slightly tougher version of buk choy. It was developed to grow close to the ground so it is easily protected from frost. The tougher larger leaves can be used, cooked, in soups and stir-fries, while the younger, smaller leaves can be eaten raw in salads. Available from Asian food stores and good greengrocers; tatsoi has a very short shelf life, so use immediately.

THAI CHILLI JAM a sweet, sourish tangy jam sold in jars at supermarkets and Asian food stores.

TOFU also known as bean curd, an off-white, custard-like product made from the "milk" of crushed soya beans; comes fresh as soft or firm, and processed as fried or pressed dried sheets. Leftover fresh tofu can be refrigerated in water (changed daily) for up to 4 days.

TOM YUM SOUP MIX a packaged dried soup mix requiring rehydration with liquid to produce a soup similar to Thailand's well-known hot and sour prawn soup.

TOMATOES, SEMI-DRIED partially dried tomato pieces in olive oil; softer and juicier than sun-dried, these are not a preserve, so do not keep as long as sun-dried.

VEAL ESCALOPES thinly sliced veal steak available plain (uncrumbed) or crumbed; we use plain (uncrumbed) in our recipes unless stated otherwise.

VINEGAR

balsamic originally from Modena, Italy, and made from the juice of Trebbiano grapes; it is a deep rich brown colour with a sweet and sour flavour.

red wine based on fermented red wine.

WATERCRESS also known as winter rocket; one of the cress family, a large group of peppery greens used raw in salads or cooked in soups. Highly perishable, so must be used as soon as possible after purchase.

ZUCCHINI also known as courgette; small green, yellow or white vegetable belonging to the squash family.

conversion chart

MEASURES

One Australian metric measuring cup holds approximately 250ml; one Australian metric tablespoon holds 20ml; one Australian metric teaspoon holds 5ml.

The difference between one country's measuring cups and another's is within a two- or three-teaspoon variance, and will not affect your cooking results. North America, New Zealand and the United Kingdom use a 15ml tablespoon.

All cup and spoon measurements are level. The most accurate way of measuring dry ingredients is to weigh them. When measuring liquids, use a clear glass or plastic jug with the metric markings.

We use large eggs with an average weight of 60g.

DRY MEASURES

METRIC	IMPERIAL
15g	½oz
30g	1oz
60g	2oz
90g	3oz
125g	4oz (¼lb)
155g	5oz
185g	6oz
220g	7oz
250g	8oz (½lb)
280g	9oz
315g	10oz
345g	11oz
375g	12oz (¾lb)
410g	13oz
440g	14oz
470g	15oz
500g	16oz (1lb)
750g	24oz (1½lb)
1kg	32oz (2lb)

LIQUID MEASURES

METRIC	IMPERIAL
30ml	1 fluid oz
60ml	2 fluid oz
100ml	3 fluid oz
125ml	4 fluid oz
150ml	5 fluid oz (¼ pint/1 gill)
190ml	6 fluid oz
250ml	8 fluid oz
300ml	10 fluid oz (½ pint)
500ml	16 fluid oz
600ml	20 fluid oz (1 pint)
1000ml (1 litre)	1¾ pints

LENGTH MEASURES

METRIC	IMPERIAL
3mm	⅛in
6mm	¼in
1cm	½in
2cm	¾in
2.5cm	1in
5cm	2in
6cm	2½in
8cm	3in
10cm	4in
13cm	5in
15cm	6in
18cm	7in
20cm	8in
23cm	9in
25cm	10in
28cm	11in
30cm	12in (1ft)

OVEN TEMPERATURES

These oven temperatures are only a guide for conventional ovens. For fan-forced ovens, check the manufacturer's manual.

	°C (CELSIUS)	°F (FAHRENHEIT)	GAS MARK
Very slow	120	250	½
Slow	150	275-300	1-2
Moderately slow	160	325	3
Moderate	180	350-375	4-5
Moderately hot	200	400	6
Hot	220	425-450	7-8
Very hot	240	475	9

index

If you like this cookbook, you'll love these...

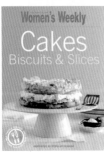

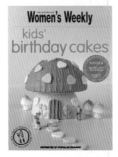

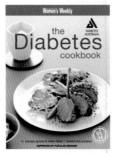

These are just a small selection of titles available in
The Australian Women's Weekly range on sale at selected
newsagents, supermarkets or online at www.acpbooks.com.au

also available in bookstores...

ACP BOOKS

General manager Christine Whiston
Editorial director Susan Tomnay
Creative director & designer Hieu Chi Nguyen
Senior editor Wendy Bryant
Text Kitchen food director Pamela Clark
Test Kitchen manager + nutritional information Belinda Farlow
Recipe development Amal Webster, Cathie Lonnie,
Mandy Sinclair, Rebecca Squadrito
Director of sales Brian Cearnes
Marketing manager Bridget Cody
Senior business analyst Rebecca Varela
Operations manager David Scotto
Production manager Victoria Jefferys
International rights enquiries Laura Bamford; lbamford@acpuk.com

ACP Books are published by ACP Magazines a division of
PBL Media Pty Limited
Publishing director, Women's lifestyle Pat Ingram
Director of sales, Women's lifestyle Lynette Phillips
Commercial manager, Women's lifestyle Seymour Cohen
Marketing director, Women's lifestyle Matthew Dominello
Public relations manager, Women's lifestyle Hannah Deveraux
Research director, Women's lifestyle Justin Stone
PBL Media, Chief Executive Officer Ian Law

Published by ACP Books, a division of ACP Magazines Ltd,
54 Park St, Sydney; GPO Box 4088, Sydney, NSW 2001.
phone (02) 9282 8618; fax (02) 9267 9438;
acpbooks@acpmagazines.com.au; www.acpbooks.com.au

Printed by Dai Nippon in Korea.

Australia Distributed by Network Services, phone +61 2 9282 8777;
fax +61 2 9264 3278; networkweb@networkservicescompany.com.au
United Kingdom Distributed by Australian Consolidated Press (UK),
phone (01604) 642 200; fax (01604) 642 300; books@acpuk.com
New Zealand Distributed by Netlink Distribution Company,
phone (9) 366 9966; ask@ndc.co.nz
South Africa Distributed by PSD Promotions,
phone (27 11) 392 6065/6/7; fax (27 11) 392 6079/80;
orders@psdprom.co.za
Canada Distributed by Publishers Group Canada
phone (800) 663 5714; fax (800) 565 3770; service@raincoast.com

Title: Short & fast / food director, Pamela Clark.
ISBN: 9 781 86396 860 7 (pbk.)
Subjects: 1 Cookery. Quick and easy cookery.
Other Authors/Contributors: Clark, Pamela.
Dewey Number: 641.555
© ACP Magazines Ltd 2009
ABN 18 053 273 546
This publication is copyright. No part of it may be reproduced or
transmitted in any form without the written permission of the publishers.

Scanpan cookware is used in the AWW Test Kitchen.
The publishers would like to thank the following for props used
in photography: Robert Gordon Australia, Accoutrement.
To order books, phone 136 116 (within Australia).
Send recipe enquiries to:
recipeenquiries@acpmagazines.com.au